Don Williams

RING OF TRUTH
A Translator's Testimony

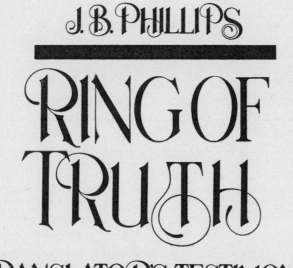

J. B. PHILLIPS

RING OF TRUTH

A TRANSLATOR'S TESTIMONY

HAROLD SHAW PUBLISHERS
WHEATON, ILLINOIS

Harold Shaw Publishers edition, 1977,
published by special arrangement with
Hodder & Stoughton, Ltd. Sevenoaks, Kent.
No part of this book may be
used or reproduced in any manner whatsoever
without written permission from the
publisher, except in the case of brief
quotations embodied in critical articles
and reviews.
For information, address Harold Shaw Publishers,
Box 567, Wheaton, Illinois 60187.

ISBN 0-87788-724-1
Library of Congress Catalog Card Number 77-80627
Printed in the United States of America

Acknowledgments

I feel I must record my gratitude to all people, young and old, who have written to me from many parts of the world. They, and the many friends with whom I have had personal conversations and discussions have helped and encouraged me, possibly without knowing it, to write this short book. I think it is those who have borne suffering with radiant faith who have above all renewed and deepened my own convictions.

To all these people it seems only fair to me to record my heartfelt gratitude.

I am also grateful to the Editor of the *Church Times* for permission to quote the letter on pp. 114–116.

Swanage, Dorset   J. B. PHILLIPS

CONTENTS

AUTHOR'S PREFACE TO THIS EDITION

I SHOULD probably never have written this book at all if I had not suffered a long period of ill-health with its attendant depression and temptation to despair. In the ordinary way I should have laughed off much of the so-called "new Christianity", and, to be plain, I should simply not have seen certain television programmes because I should have been conducting a service in church. But all suffering brings us into contact with fellow-sufferers, and from letters, conversations and telephone calls I began to realise how the foundations of the faith were apparently being eroded by the clever intellectuals who write and speak with such assurance. Were I not sure of God, and were I not sure of the basic integrity of the documents which I had translated, I could easily imagine how my own faith could have been undermined.

Thus I wrote, often under very difficult circumstances. The book was deliberately simple, and it was deliberately first published at the cheapest possible price. Of course I have simplified some of the issues involved, but this is not to be understood as meaning that I am unaware of them. I have nowhere suppressed or altered the basic truth in which I believe.

To "walk by faith", which is what we have to do in this life, is never easy, and I therefore decided to set down my

9

own simple testimony in order to help others. The response has astonished me. I have not had one hostile letter: on the contrary the book has been fervently welcomed by a very wide variety of people. I have no objection to confirming the faith of the old and frail, but the interesting thing to me is that many of the letters come from those in the prime of life, some of whom have intellectual qualifications much higher than mine. I have therefore made a selection from some of these and, at my publisher's request, the relevant parts are printed in this edition of the book.

First of all, here is part of a letter from a young Divinity student in this country, personally quite unknown to me:

"I feel that I must write to you to express my very real thanks for the help and encouragement that *Ring of Truth* has given to me and that I am sure it will give to many more people.

"I am a Divinity student at a College of Education and to some extent therefore a specialist and I too have been appalled by the way in which many of the 'experts' have spoken publicly about their doubts and by their lack of discretion have destroyed or severely shaken the faith of many young Christians, some of whom are known to me.

"Thank you for your courage in speaking out against such indiscretion, but thank you also for the remainder of the book which in a positive way acts as a very wonderful handbook to the New Testament, and a very stimulating and refreshing aid in meeting a real and living Christ through its pages."

And here is part of a letter from a group of students at a college in Scotland, not noted for ultra-conservatism:

"Just a very brief note – from a few of us here – in appreciation of your recent publication – the little paperback *Ring of Truth*. Your spiritual discernment, coupled to a deep sense of humility, makes your thesis ring with notes of conviction and joy. At a time when the central truths of our faith are being subject to cynicism in every area of society – and particularly from the supposedly mature insights of some of the leading philosophical and theological thinkers of our age – it gives tremendous encouragement to hear again the call of intregrity, grounded in the triumph of Calvary ...

"Many theological students in this country, in Europe and in the States – convinced that a spiritual awakening is the one certain hope for the races of the earth – will find your opinions and ideas both a challenge and an inspiration."

After these, which serve to underline the conversations I have had with young people who are concerned by the scepticism of those who are supposed to be instructing them in the Christian faith, I now quote an extract from a schoolmaster who teaches religious instruction and biology:

"This is a short but very sincere expression of thanks to you for your recent book *Ring of Truth*. It came into my hands at a most effective moment, and with an impressive relevance. As a master in a Grammar School I am responsible for sixth-form R.I. and Biology ... I read to the class as much as could be conveniently covered in the period available. The reading commanded the attention and respect of these senior pupils, and has given valuable affirmation to the facts that I had put before them."

This view is further upheld by an eminent Professor of Biology:

"I think this is a wonderful book, and I can say, without reserve that I agree with every statement in it. I particularly admire its clarity. It would be difficult to find a book on the same topics which is so free from obscurities."

Again I turn to the teaching profession, and that means to me those who feel a responsibility for the minds of those whom they are trying to teach:

"For my alive sixth-form boys and girls this book will hold them, for

they are enormously interested. We have several sets of your paperbacks . . .
No other books have helped me, as a Teacher of R.E. in a Grammar School,
so much and now *Ring of Truth* will be added."

But there are others concerned, even though they may
be labelled as "do-gooders". These words from a welfare
worker cheered me greatly:

"It is like a breath of fresh air in these days, with the trend to mytholo-
gise Holy Scripture and all the confusion and lowering of standards that
trail in its wake.

"We are to make *Ring of Truth* our March book of the month. To
Christians both mature in and on the brink of the Christian faith, it will be
the book of the year."

The next extract comes from a young housewife and
mother who, some years ago, was a member of my youth
club:

"For my part your new book has completely dispelled the anguish I felt
when I read *Honest to God* and which lurked at the back of my mind for
several years. That book caused me to kneel in tears on Easter evening after
a particularly beautiful service, and wonder if all I had believed and tried
to follow for years was in vain. Although *Honest to God* may have done some
good in causing people to think about their faith, I am sure it also upset
a lot of Christian people more than was necessary."

I began to hear from the "dignitaries", people whose
intellectual capacity is certainly greater than mine. The
first is from a Diocesan Bishop:

"I feel I must write immediately to thank you from the bottom of my
heart for your magnificent book. If ever a publication was timely it is your
book and I thank God for you and for all that you have meant to the Church
throughout the years and in particular I thank God for your courage in

saying all that you have said in this book. It will do much to rally drooping spirits and to infuse new life and optimism into the Church."

Then, from another Bishop, whose mind is razor-sharp though he has recently retired from active diocesan work:

"It is a timely affirmation of sober sense which will help to reassure thousands."

Then, quite unexpectedly came a few words from Oxford, from one of the most brilliant minds we have living today:

"I am delighted with your book. It cannot fail to be of interest because of the living and personal way you have set out true experiences."

This was endorsed quite independently by another expert in the field of Divinity, who lectures on the New Testament in one of our biggest universities:

"I am delighted at the positive line you are taking in your writings. How depressing a lot of recent publications have been – and how unnecessarily so. May your writings, with the divine blessing, help to turn the tide."

But I found it was not only the experts in Divinity who welcomed what I had written. Here is part of a letter from one who is unquestionably a leading expert in the field of psychiatry:

"I read it through at a sitting ... and thought that, once again, you had demonstrated that unique capacity of yours for stating the experiences which many of us have in our religion and making clear to us the roots of our faith and why we are justified in preserving these in our simple, traditional way."

And then, among letters from many others who, I

suppose, are highly intelligent but not intellectual, I received the following from a district nurse who, like a parish priest, sees people in all kinds of trouble and affliction:

"Thank you for writing *Ring of Truth*. Being of the number of 'little ones' it is heartening to me to find my innermost conviction given expression in this way. . . . In writing this I am sure I only echo the opinion of thousands; and being a district nurse in this place, I know how troubled some people are by the pronouncements of learned talkers. While I believe God protects His 'poor' with an intuitive sense of truth, it is good to have the support of sound and informed reason."

Here is a further extract, this time from one of the Moderators of the Congregational Church:

"It is helpful to have something with the ring of conviction about it in days when the faith is so often spoken about in a negative and tentative way. We are in an unhappy plight when only the extreme fundamentalists can speak with certainty in their voice. You have taken the initiative on behalf of a more liberal and informed reading of the N.T. with what A. S. Eddington called 'a sureness which is very different from cocksureness', and I think many good Christians who have been helped by your earlier work, will 'thank God and take courage'."

Where the truth about Christ is concerned denominational barriers are irrelevant. A scholar, not an Anglican, wrote from the Midlands:

"I am delighted to have a copy of *Ring of Truth*. I read this with great appreciation and complete agreement. This will be of great help to many people who are bewildered by some of the sceptical nonsense that is being talked and written at the moment. Coming as it does from someone who has steeped himself in the New Testament it carries a weight and an authority which few other writers can command.

I felt like raising a cheer when I came to the end, because it ties up so closely with my own views after more than twenty years' teaching and writing. I get very impatient with the attention that is paid to radicals who seem to me to be intentionally or unintentionally trying to destroy rather than to build up."

And one of the leading figures in the Salvation Army, who is not only very well-read but has a deeper knowledge of human nature than most scholars, wrote to me these words:

"I would like to thank you most sincerely for a copy of your latest book *Ring of Truth*. I have almost completed reading this and feel that it is a very much needed contribution at this present time. One of the most perplexing aspects of our present situation is that the attempt to help some proves a positive hindrance to others. I myself feel that some of the modern theologians have been so concerned to communicate with modern man that they have cut themselves off from their own roots as it were. I believe that a necessary balancing of their more extreme interpretations is now beginning to be made."

A former B.B.C. producer who has a brilliantly acute mind wrote these words:

"I am delighted to have this. It seems to me one of the best things you have written, and it comes like a breath of fresh air blowing through this rather murky atmosphere of debate."

Then as a bolt from the blue came a letter from a Scottish divine who possesses more degrees than I am ever likely to gain:

"May I say 'Thank you very much' for *Ring of Truth*. I know . . . and his friends of the sloppy morality are wrong but had been able to say so only in the most blundering of terms and, of course, without the enormous prestige of your own scholarly achievements."

From just south of the border came another letter, again from someone whose intellectual capacity I greatly respect:

"I was very grateful to receive *Ring of Truth* which I think is a splendid book, and needed writing. To anyone who uses their heart as well as their head it is completely convincing, and I imagine it will have a vast and life-giving sale."

A grateful letter from the Principal of a Training College in the south:

"I have read and re-read it and felt that I must write and express my gratitude to you. For most of my teaching career I have been concerned with Divinity for the ordinary pupils and students: and the experience of this has been a steadily growing conviction of the reliability of the Gospels."

And so I could go on. But, apart from the distinguished and the intellectual there have been scores of ordinary folk who have written to express their enormous relief that someone of my so-called "eminence" should have given the testimony I have. They all express refreshment and reinforcement in the Faith which they felt was being whittled away by those who, they think, are our "leaders" and "thinkers".

Here are some typical extracts:

"I have found it most helpful, stimulating and comforting. Without doubt it will prove a great blessing to many hundreds of readers. . . . It is high time, in this modern world, that someone stood up boldly, for the truth, when religion is treated as necessary or unnecessary pop entertainment of little consequence, one way, or another."

"You will never know the help you have brought to the common foot-soldier of the struggling Christian Army of today, but odd words of thanks may uphold you. *Ring of Truth* is just the book so many of us were waiting for."

"I am not in the habit of writing to complete strangers but I felt I must write to thank you very much indeed for your book *Ring of Truth*. One is continually bombarded on T.V. and in books by learned people, all more or less saying that Christianity is a myth. Last year, just before Easter, I read *The Passover Plot* and it really upset me. I attended the Easter services but wondering all the time if there were any sense in it. After reading your book – twice over – I feel happy again."

These are only a few of a constant stream of letters; they come from all denominations, including the Roman Catholic Church. They confirm in my own mind the strong impression that, while we may well have to alter our language, our methods and our presentation of the everlasting Gospel, there are a great many people who are convinced, as I am, that the Christian faith is rooted in history, and that the living Spirit of God is as alive and powerful as ever.

FOREWORD

I DO NOT write for scholars; they can look after themselves. For twenty-five years I have written for the ordinary man who is no theologian. Alas, today, he frequently gets the impression that the New Testament is no longer historically reliable.

What triggered off my anger (righteous, I trust) against some of our "experts" is this. A clergyman, old, retired, useless if you like, took his own life because his reading of the "new theology" and even some programmes on television, finally drove him, in his loneliness and ill-health, to conclude that his own life's work had been founded upon a lie. He felt that these highly-qualified writers and speakers must know so much more than he that they must be right. Jesus Christ did not really rise from the dead and the New Testament, on which he had based his life and ministry, was no more than a bundle of myths.

That made me angry, and I remembered the terrible words of Jesus which, in effect, say that a man would be better off dead than cause one of "his little ones to stumble". For many years it has been my solid purpose to communicate the truth of the Christian Gospel. I am *not* concerned to distort or dilute the Christian faith so that modern undergraduates, for example, can accept it without a murmur. I am concerned with the truth revealed in and through Jesus Christ. Let the modern world conform to him, and never let us dare to try to make him fit into our clever-clever modern world. I am no anti-intellectual, any more than St. Paul, who wrote so penetratingly that "the world by wisdom knew not God". But I say quite bluntly that some of the intellectuals (by no means all, thank God!), who write so cleverly and devastatingly about the Christian faith appear to have no personal knowledge of the living God. For they lack awe, they lack humility, and they lack the responsibility which every Christian owes to his weaker brother. They make sure they are never made "fools for Christ's sake", however many people's faith they may undermine.

Few people have had such a close and constant contact with the New Testament as I have. Even fewer have taken the trouble to understand the business of "communication". I say this in no spirit of conceit; it is a matter of simple fact. I therefore felt that it was high time that someone, who has spent the best years of his life in studying both the New Testament and good modern communicative English, spoke out. I do not care a rap what the "*avant-garde*" scholars say; I do very much care what God says and does. I have therefore felt compelled to write this book. It is my testimony to the historicity and reliability of the New Testament.

J. B. PHILLIPS

1. The Truth of Experience

IN a recent book* the Revd. Harry Williams, Dean of Trinity College, Cambridge, draws attention to the two kinds of truth which face us as human beings. One is the "outside" sort, which means the knowledge of ascertained facts in whatever department of human activity we are involved but which is outside our own personalities. The other kind of truth to which Mr. Williams draws our attention is the "inside" truth. This is the truth we know within ourselves, in part intuitively and in part as a result of experience. It grows out of fear, disappointment and doubt as well as out of joy, conviction and confident faith. Indeed Mr. Williams goes so far as to suggest, tentatively at least, that there might be a kind of theology of this inner self.

I believe that such a "theology" might answer several very important questions. What is it, for example, that lives within the spirit of a man which enables him to detect truth, even though it may prove painful and destructive to his previous illusions? Here lies one of life's great mysteries. What God-given faculty is it that enables us to recognise the Word of God as the Word of God and not

* *The True Wilderness* (Constable).

as a mere human opinion or doctrine? Of course the moment we accept the Christian belief that all men are, at least potentially, the sons of God there is at least the beginning of an explanation. Why should not the son recognise, however faintly, the true tone of his Father's voice?

From my own experience, that is from my own knowledge of my own inner truth, I believe this recognition of God's word to be a valid part of human experience. And when I find, as I have done over the last thirty years, that this inner experience is shared by thousands in various parts of the world, I am convinced that here is an authentic part of human existence which is all too often ignored. It is not so much that the bare Word speaks to us from the New Testament out of context (although, of course, it sometimes does that), as that what God has to say through the inspired writers sheds a quite unique light upon human living and dying.

THE POWER OF THE WORD

I have said that the bare Word sometimes speaks to a man quite out of context, and that fact can be verified from the records of the Bible Society. Without any human intermediary a Gospel or even a verse from a Gospel can speak to any man reading it in his own tongue for the first time. The result is not infrequently dramatic: a man's whole attitude to life may be changed. God has spoken to him and he is (in the New Testament sense) converted. I cannot give individual examples without breaking confidences, but I have plenty of evidence in my files of this kind of thing. I am not thinking of people whose upbringing was steeped in biblical teaching and who then, after years of rebellion and evasion, were challenged by being confronted by a truth which was in fact part of their childhood's training. Of course that does happen, but I am thinking of men and women of various nationalities who had no Christian indoctrination in their early years and had never read the New Testament in their lives before. Yet their way of living was altered fundamentally when God spoke to them through these writings.

EVADING THE CHALLENGE

But having said this, it does not seem to me a common thing for a mere "text" to challenge, still less convert, anyone. Yet a close study of the remarkable collection of books which are known as the New Testament can, and constantly does, challenge, provoke and appeal to a man at a deeper level and with a more profound authority than any other human writing. Human beings can easily insulate themselves from any shock or disturbance of this kind by simply not reading it. So long as a man confines his ideas of Christ to a rather misty hero-figure of long ago who died a tragic death, and so long as his ideas of Christianity are bounded by what he calls the Sermon on the Mount (which he has almost certainly not read in its entirety since he became grown-up), then the living truth never has a chance to touch him. This is plainly what has happened to many otherwise intelligent people. Over the years I have had hundreds of conversations with people, many of them of higher intellectual calibre than my own, who quite obviously had no idea of what Christianity is really about. I was in no case trying to catch them out; I was simply and gently trying to find out what they knew about the New Testament. My conclusion was that they knew virtually nothing. This I find pathetic and somewhat horrifying. It means that the most important Event in human history is politely and quietly by-passed. For it is not as though the evidence had been examined and found unconvincing; it had simply never been examined.

Apart from sheer neglect, the other way in which human beings can protect themselves from the rather frightening vitality of the New Testament is by carefully dismembering it. It is obviously right that we should have New Testament scholars — indeed I owe much to them — but it is horribly possible so to dissect your subject that you remove its life. By the time each source and component has been tagged and labelled this vibrant and compelling body of writing is no more than a cadaver on the theological operating-table.

THE EXPERTS' RESPONSIBILITY

Although I know personally several excellent New Testament scholars who would certainly regard the material of their study with the utmost reverence, it is worth pointing out how criticisms by experts percolate through to the non-expert as detrimental and destructive. Perhaps this is unavoidable in our modern society, but I cannot forget Christ's stern words about "causing one of his little ones to stumble", or Paul's warning about "the weaker brother". We who have grown into a strong and mature faith must surely regard it as part of our responsibility to do or say nothing which would undermine faith. I believe this to be especially binding upon us in the fields of mass communication. What can profitably be discussed between men of many years' Christian experience may be quite unsuitable for a television programme, which may be seen by the weak, the fearful, the lonely and the dying. I make no plea for obscurantism. Those who know me as a parish priest will agree that I have always taken the line that if the Christian faith can be destroyed by somebody or other's clever-clever talk it cannot be basically very strong. But the broadcaster, and perhaps especially the solo television speaker, enjoys an almost *ex cathedra* position of non-contradiction. I am convinced that he has no right to air his own doubts and fancies as though they were matters of agreed faith among Christians.

RELIGION-LESS CHRISTIANITY

Various theological ideas have nowadays percolated through to ordinary people, and their effect has been to make them even less ready than before to read the New

Testament with serious adult attention. Such phrases as "religion-less Christianity" are bandied about as though we had outgrown God. But if we read even the paperback *Letters and Papers from Prison* by the Christian martyr Dietrich Bonhoeffer, to whom the phrase is attributed, it is obvious that he did not mean anything of the kind. He was protesting, and rightly, against religion divorced from life — and what true Christian wouldn't? — but he was a deeply religious man to the day of his death. Nevertheless the phrase sticks. The modern humanist with his irrational prejudice against anything "supernatural" welcomes the idea of a sort of Christianity without religion. But, of course, true Christianity is rooted in both God and man. The New Testament gives no sort of endorsement to modern man's extraordinary illusion of being able to dispense with God.

DE-MYTHOLOGISING

Further, we have the percolated influence of another German theologian, Rudolf Bultmann. His idea, which amounts to an obsession, is that "the life of Jesus is set in such a mythological framework that its real meaning can only be found when we get rid of the whole first-century background".* I believe that this idea is almost wholly false. But what happens to the idea when it filters through to the general people? Simply the impression that leading theologians and New Testament scholars all regard the

* Quoting William Neil, *The Life and Teaching of Jesus* (Hodder and Stoughton).

stories of Jesus as "myths". And, make no mistake, that means to the ordinary man and woman that they are no more than concocted stories with about as much truth in them as the fables of Æsop and with about as much authority as the myth of Father Christmas. It would not be true to say that Bultmann and his very considerable following have any difficulty in combining their sceptical view of the historicity of the Gospels with a real devotion to the faith of the Church. But this demands an agility and dexterity which escapes me. All that I am concerned with is the effect of the Bultmann "de-mythologisation" upon ordinary non-theologically trained people.

FIRST-HAND CONTACT

The New Testament, given a fair hearing, does not need me or anyone else to defend it. It has the proper ring for anyone who has not lost his ear for truth. But because in these days it has been compromised in the eyes of many people by those who should know better, I feel I can do no other than record my own impressions as honestly and faithfully as I can. As the years have passed – and it is now twenty-five years since I began translating the "Epistles" – my conviction has grown that the New Testament is in a quite special sense inspired. It is not magical, nor is it faultless: human beings wrote it. But by something which I would not hesitate to describe as a miracle, there is a concentration upon that area of inner truth which is fundamental and ageless. That, I believe, is the

27

reason why millions of people have heard the voice of God speaking to them through these seemingly artless pages.

PERSONAL CONVICTIONS

But before I begin my testimony as a translator I must make a few reservations. First, although I believe in the true inspiration of the New Testament and its obvious power to change human lives in this or any other century, I should like to make it quite clear that I could not possibly hold the extreme "fundamentalist" position of so-called "verbal inspiration". This theory is bound to break down sooner or later in the world of translation. There are over eleven hundred known human languages, and it was during a brief spell of work for the British and Foreign Bible Society that I learned of the attempts to translate the Bible, or at least parts of it, into nearly all of these different tongues. I learned of the extreme ingenuity which the translator must use to convey sense and truth where word-for-word transmission is out of the question. You cannot talk to tribes who live without ever seeing navigable water of our possessing "an anchor for the soul". You cannot speak to the Eskimos of "the Lamb of God which taketh away the sin of the world", or of Christ being "the true Vine" and of us, his disciples, as "the branches"! Such examples could, literally, be multiplied many thousands of times. Yet I have found, when addressing meetings in this country and in America, that there still survives a minority who passionately believe in verbal inspiration. It appears that they have never seriously thought that there are millions for whom Christ died who would find a word-for-word translation of the New Testament, even if it were possible, frequently meaningless. Any man who has sense as well as faith is bound to conclude that it is the *truths* which are inspired and not the words which are merely the vehicles of truth.

Secondly, although I have no wish to deny the great truths embodied in that tremendous book of celestial poetry which we call the Book of Revelation, the general remarks which follow cannot be applied to that book. It is part of the New Testament, and I have no quarrel with those who included it in the sacred canon. I am only concerned here to say that it does stand in a special place and demands very special consideration.*

Thirdly, I had no intention of putting my version forward in some kind of competition with the beauty and majesty of the Authorised Version of 1611. I undertook the task of translation chiefly for the sake of the young people at that time under my care in wartime London. I suppose that like many another clergyman or minister I had never realised what a barrier beautiful but antique words had imposed.

THE BEGINNING OF MY WORK

I began, then, with the Epistles, or Letters, of Paul. I felt that while most of the people to whom I was

* For those who are interested may I recommend my own Preface to *The Book of Revelation* (Bles or Fontana).

ministering had at least a nodding acquaintance with the Gospels, the Epistles were to them forbidding and "difficult". We were, like several millions in London, Christians in danger, and since much of the message of the New Testament Epistles is addressed to Christians in danger, I felt that here was an additional reason for putting them into English which could readily be understood.

It was not easy in those wartime days to set aside even a few hours a week for this work. I had very few books with me, and (as those who are old enough will remember) it was virtually impossible to get others – quite impossible if they were printed abroad. But I had a rare stroke of good fortune for which I am still grateful. I sent a copy of my version of "Colossians" (reprinted from a local Parish Magazine) to the late C. S. Lewis. He replied with great encouragement. He wrote – "It's like seeing an old picture after it's been cleaned", and that is a sentence which I remember and treasure, especially as that was precisely the effect I was trying to produce. A little later Lewis suggested that I should translate all the New Testament Epistles and it was he who suggested the excellent title, *Letters to Young Churches.*

THE RELEASE OF TRUTH

The first effect of my work astonished me. The people for whom I had made this translation began to see, and sometimes saw quite suddenly, the relevance of these Letters to life. The removal of the old varnish allowed the truth to reach them in a way it had not reached them before. The second effect was upon me, the translator. I found, as I have written elsewhere, that once one gets to grips with the actual stuff of the New Testament, its vitality is astonishing. I found myself provoked, challenged, stimulated, comforted and generally convicted of my previous shallow knowledge of Holy Scripture. The centuries seemed to melt away and here was I confronted by eternal truths which my soul, however reluctantly, felt bound to accept. The further I went on with my work of translation the more this conviction of spiritual truth grew within me.

— AND ITS ASTONISHING VITALITY

I must, in common justice, confess here that for years I had viewed the Greek of the New Testament with a rather snobbish disdain. I had read the best of Classical Greek both at school and Cambridge for over ten years. To come down to the *Koine* of the first century A.D. seemed, as I have sometimes remarked rather uncharitably, like reading Shakespeare for some years and then turning to the Vicar's letter in the Parish Magazine! But I think now that I was wrong: I can see that the expression of the Word of God in ordinary workaday language is all of a piece with God's incredible humility in becoming Man in Jesus Christ. And, further, the language itself is not so pedestrian as I had at first supposed. Although I did my utmost to preserve an emotional detachment I found again and again that the material under my hands was strangely alive; it spoke to my condition in the most uncanny way. I say "uncanny" for want of a better word, but it was a very strange experience to sense, not occasionally but almost continually, the living quality of those rather strangely assorted books. To me it is the more remarkable because I had no fundamentalist up-bringing, and although as a priest of the Anglican Church I had a great respect for Holy Scripture, this very close contact of several years of translation produced an effect of "inspiration" which I have never experienced, even in the remotest degree, in any other work.

THE "OLD SCRIPTURE" BECAME NEW

I found this sense of inspiration highly communicable. Once the language difficulty was removed the Letters spoke for themselves. In the world of Paul, John, Peter and James we were in a world to many people as yet un-explored. The little stories of Jesus, half-remembered from Sunday School, and the unrealistic mental images which tender minds had absorbed of "Gentle Jesus meek and mild" were no longer appropriate. For the real world of the first century A.D. was tough and cruel, and the Christians who lived in it had to be real people, utterly convinced of their faith, utterly devoted to the Lord whom most of them had never seen. Their struggles, their en-durance, their strength of purpose in the face of appalling odds seemed to us in those days of World War II to have an extraordinary relevance. The intervening centuries might never have been; inspired words took on a new and, so to speak, contemporary authority. Indeed so great was this sense of contemporaneity that we had constantly to remind ourselves of the different conditions of those early days: the danger and difficulties of travel, the uncertainties of communication and the lack of almost every modern "amenity". Further, there was a threat which loomed over these early Christian communities, the ever-present possibility of persecution and even of death. It is true that we were again and again threatened with death or mutilation by bombs from the German air force, but the sharing of common danger is not comparable with the persecution of a minority. Yet the spells of acute danger which we endured brought home to us the magnificent and joyful resilience of early Christianity. I can remember, for example, a particularly dangerous time, when we were officially urged not to have large groups of people assembled together. I used to conduct short services in people's houses or in air-raid shelters. Again and again passages from Paul's letters could scarcely have been more apt. One particular truth I tried to see then, and urged others to accept, is contained in Paul's words: *"in* all these things we are more than conquerors". (Rom. 8: 37). We often think that eventually all will be well (and so it will), but Paul's point is that *in the midst* of cold and hunger, of danger to life and limb, we are more than conquerors.

2. The Truth of the Letters

WHEN I started translating some of Paul's shorter letters
I was at first alternately stimulated and annoyed by the
outrageous certainty of his faith. It was not until I realised
afresh what the man had actually achieved, and suffered,
that I began to see that here was someone who was
writing, not indeed at God's dictation, but by the inspiration of God himself. Sometimes you can see the
conflicts between the pharisaic spirit of the former Saul
(who could say such grudging things about marriage
and insist upon the perennial submission of women),
and the Spirit of God who inspired Paul to write that
in Christ there is neither "Jew nor Greek . . . male nor
female"!

Paul had, and still has, his detractors. There are those
who say he is like the man who says "I don't want to boast,
but—", and then proceeds to do that very thing! Very
well then, but let us look at his list of "boasting". We
have only to turn up 2 Corinthians 11: 23–27. Have any
of us gone through a tenth of that catalogue of suffering
and humiliation? Yet this is the man who can not only say
that in all these things we are more than conquerors, but
can also "reckon that the sufferings of this present time

are not worthy to be compared with the glory which shall be revealed in us". (Rom. 8: 18). Here is no armchair philosopher, no ivory-tower scholar, but a man of almost incredible drive and courage, living out in actual human dangers and agonies the implications of his unswerving faith.

PAUL'S LETTER TO CORINTH

But the Letter which really struck me a blow from which I have never recovered was the one popularly known as "First Corinthians". Let me explain. I had been doing some background reading, and I was reminded that Corinth was a by-word, even in those wicked old days, for every kind of vice and depravity. The Greeks, as usual, had a word for it, and "to Corinthise yourself" was to live with the candle alight at both ends, with all scruples and principles thrown aside, and every desire indulged to the full. Because of its geographical position – Corinth was easily reached by sea, and was a most important port in the East–West Mediterranean traffic – it had a very mixed population with a large number of travellers, traders and hangers-on. It was probably not intrinsically any more wicked than any other sea-port, but its reputation for sexual licence had largely grown because it had been for hundreds of years a centre for the organised worship of the goddess of Love (first Aphrodite and now in Roman times, Venus). As always happens where there is such widespread sexual licence, there sprang up a host of vicious fellow-travellers — greed, blackmail, cheating, slander, perversion and the rest.

I had a fair picture of the sort of place it must have been, and indeed of what an unlikely place it must have seemed for the founding of a Christian church, when I suddenly came across 1 Corinthians 6: 11. Paul has just recounted some of the more repulsive sins to which human beings can sink and has assured his hearers that the Kingdom of God cannot be the possession of people like that, when suddenly he writes, AND SUCH WERE SOME OF YOU!

EVIDENCE OF SOMETHING SUPER-HUMAN

I had never realised what an astonishing piece of Christian evidence this is. No one doubts that this is an authentic Letter of Paul, probably written some ten years before the first Gospel was set down. And here, to people living in this centre of idolatry and all kinds of human depravity Paul can write "and such were some of you"! What, I ask, and shall continue to ask of my non-Christian friends, is supposed to have changed these men and women so fundamentally? The personality of Paul? The most casual reading of his two surviving Letters to Corinth will quickly show that even among his converts he was not universally admired. It seemed obvious that something very unusual had happened and was happening. People, sometimes the most unlikely people, were being converted in heart and mind by *something*. To Paul and his fellow apostles it was plainly the invasion of the human spirit by God's own Spirit. The power required to convert and to sustain the new life *naturally*, was to Paul another manifestation of the power which God showed in raising Jesus from the dead. The "fruits of the Spirit" which Paul lists in the fifth chapter of his Letter to the Galatians are not the result of fearful effort and tormenting self-denial. They are fruits: they grow naturally, once the living Spirit of God is allowed to enter a man's inner being.

Here then, are two miracles: the transformation of human nature from within and the raising of the man Jesus from death. According to Paul's Gospel they are both demonstrations of God's power in the midst of human circumstances and in spite of human probability.

I do not propose to linger long here on the well-known prose-poem about Christian love which is in the thirteenth chapter. I do not think that its authority is in question, and I will merely comment, for the benefit of those who sometimes find Paul irritating, that this must be the work of a man of rare insight and equally rare poetic genius. It is in itself a miracle that a man with the training of Saul of Tarsus should see with such clarity that without "love" every scrap of learning and achievement, every strenuous effort and every painful sacrifice amount to nothing at all.

EARLY CHRISTIAN CONVICTION

Then I came to the fifteenth chapter, which I have come to regard in some ways as the most important chapter in

the New Testament. Certainly it is the earliest evidence
for the resurrection of Christ. We need to remind ourselves that so far there were no written Gospels, and that
these words were written some twenty years after the
crucifixion of Jesus. There would still be many alive who
knew and remembered him, and Paul lists some of those
who saw Christ alive after his very public death. I was
struck again by the "over five hundred Christians" who
saw Jesus simultaneously, "of whom", Paul comments,
"the majority are still alive". The evidence of the resurrection does not rest on hysterical visions in the half-light
of early dawn but on actual "appearances", the last of
which seems to have happened to Paul. I noticed the flat,
matter-of-fact recital of known events. There is no attempt
to persuade or prove, and certainly there is no artistic
embellishment. Paul is, in effect, saying: these are the
historic facts which we know.

Then, at verse twelve, he does allow himself to be
moved. Since the risen Christ convinced him, and since
the risen Christ is the power behind the gospel he preaches,
as well as the author of the faith which has grown up in
the unlikely soil of Corinth, how *can* anyone, even for the
sake of argument, deny that Christ really rose?

I confess that I was as much astonished as Paul that
Christians should not believe in the life that is to follow
this obviously incomplete and imperfect one. During the
years of the war, when death could strike at anyone with
little or no warning, it was not thought morbid but merely
commonsense to consider what happens to us after our
bodies "die". I had several hundred conversations with

those who were bereaved, and I believe that these inspired words of long ago brought reassurance to many. We learned to accept our mortality, and our faith in Christ's promises was greatly strengthened.

But since the war ended it seems that quite a proportion of professing Christians do not really believe in any life after this temporal one. Recently I read that the 1964 Gallup Poll gave to ABC Television the following percentages:

> 88 per cent of regular Roman Catholics,
> 86 per cent of regular Non-Conformists,
> 85 per cent of regular Church of England

attenders believe in life after death. Since faith in the resurrection of Christ and the sharing of his timeless life has always been an integral part of the Gospel, I cannot help wondering why quite a proportion of those who accept Christianity stop short of its most valuable promise.

"ETERNITY" IS NOT EXTENDED TIME

It may be that there is some lack of imagination. If we speak loosely of "eternity", some people think that we mean millions of years plus millions of years *ad infinitum*. They do not seem able to grasp the fact that once we are outside the time-and-space set-up (in which we are in this life inescapably confined), neither "time" nor "space" has any meaning. There may be all kinds of "dimensions" of which we are at present ignorant, and for which there are no descriptive words.

But I believe Paul himself puts his finger on the nub of the matter in verse thirty-five on this same chapter. Some people then, as some people now, seemed to envisage this temporary corruptible body being magically revived, and to think that this is what is meant by "resurrection". Of course it is not. Paul is at pains to explain that even on this planet the "body" which contains the life is adapted to the environment – fish, birds, animals are all different, while the "celestial bodies" to be observed in the sky are completely and splendidly unlike anything earthly.

God gives us the "spiritual" body suitable for the new environment for which we are destined as sons of God. We can be sure of that, and the resurrection of Christ is our guarantee. We can be equally sure that "the transitory could never possess the everlasting". (v. 50). Indeed who would wish for this old, weary, diseased, and possibly maimed body to be somehow newly injected with life? We know perfectly well that human flesh eventually decays, quickly by fire or slowly by decomposition in the earth, whatever the "morticians" of America would have us believe.

Why then does Paul insist on a "body" at all? It is because he is concerned to defend the Christian belief in man's resurrection after the pattern of Christ's resurrection. The old Greek belief, and its Roman counterpart, held that once the body was dead the disembodied soul lived in a miserable twilight existence in Hades. It was the place of shadows and shades, the dark and joyless limbo of the departed. The Hebrew idea of Sheol was very little different. Sadness, silence and hopelessness seemed to brood over the life after death. The men and women of Corinth would probably have heard of both Hades and Sheol. They might also have heard vaguely of the Greek philosophers' concept of the immortality of the human soul.

THE ABOLITION OF DEATH

But death was to men of those days the ultimate disaster. It may be that some of these Corinthians could not accept the miserable twilight of such places as Hades or Sheol and that the persistence of the "soul" seemed no more than a philosopher's speculation. It may be that to believe in annihilation at death seemed to them the best way to meet it.

This negative thinking Paul is determined to correct. The resurrection of Christ was always to him the key to the human dilemma. Christ had become man, Christ had died for man, and Christ had risen to open the door to the glories that human vocabulary has no words to describe. Paul knew that man's last enemy, death, was now defeated, and men could look forward, not to a shadowy half-life, but to a life fuller and more glorious than human imagination can conceive. No more nonsense, he urges, about what sort of "body" we shall possess when these mortal bodies perish. That we can safely leave to God, who has demonstrated the defeat of death by the raising up of Christ.

NEW TESTAMENT CERTAINTY

For me, the translator, this fifteenth chapter seemed alive and vibrant, not with pious hope, but with inspired certainty. Quite suddenly I realised that *no man had ever written such words before*. As I pressed on with the task of translation I came to feel utterly convinced of the truth of the resurrection. Something of literally life-and-death importance had happened in mortal history, and I was reading the actual words of people who had seen Christ after his resurrection and had seen men and women deeply changed by his living power. Previously, although I had known something of the "comfort of the Scriptures" and had never thought them to be false, I must have been insulated from their reality simply because they were known as "scripture". Now I was compelled to come to the closest possible terms with this writing and I was enormously impressed, and still am. On the one hand these Letters were written over quite a period of years, but there is not the slightest discernible diminution of faith. And on the other hand it was borne in upon me with irresistible force that these Letters could never have been written at all if there had been no Jesus Christ, no crucifixion and no resurrection.

The more I thought about it, the more unthinkable it became that any of this new courageous, joyful life could have originated in any kind of concocted story or wishful thinking. There had been a stupendous Event, and from that was flowing all this strength and utter conviction.

I was, and indeed am, impressed by the fact that the New Testament letters were written not in some holy retreat but sometimes from prison, sometimes from ordinary, probably Christian, homes. Moreover, they were written to people who were called to live Christian lives in a thoroughly pagan world. Moral standards of all kinds were low and there was nothing remotely resembling a Christian public opinion. There were no Sundays, no church buildings and very little leisure for most people. Slavery was, of course, everywhere, and so were dire poverty and unrelieved sickness and disease. The great persecutions had not yet started but the smaller ones had. A man could lose not only his friends but his livelihood in a place like Ephesus if it became known publicly that he did not believe in the goddess Diana. A man could easily be looked at askance if he disowned the local gods, and he could be considered very odd if he broke with his previous companions in alcoholic revellings. And it could have been very easy to frame a charge against a man who set Jesus Christ above the Emperor of the Roman Empire.

THE VIGOUR OF THE NEW FAITH

It was against such a background of mixed paganism that the Christian faith began to grow and expand. Even if I were not myself a convinced Christian I should find it impossible to explain this strange phenomenon. If we had records of a few emotional meetings, the effects of which were merely transient, we could write the whole Christian movement off as one of those passing waves of superstition which did from time to time disturb the pagan world. But we have no such thing: we have as good solid evidence of a strong and growing faith as any historian could require. Let us, for a moment, discount the Gospel stories as written-up histories of a hero long since dead. (I do not myself think of the four Gospels like this, as I hope to show.) Even without the evidence of the books attributed to the four evangelists, we have the strongest possible evidence for the early days of Christianity from the Letters of Paul, James, Peter and John. It is *letters* which are of unique value to the historian who is trying to record the actual events of any period. Newspapers, and before them broadsheets and pamphlets, naturally have their worth, but they are likely to be slanted one way or another. But if the historian can lay his hands upon a packet of letters he has priceless evidence for the period of which he is writing. For letters, speaking generally, are not written with any political axe to grind nor are they usually written for posterity. They reflect accurately the times in which they are written.

So it is with the New Testament Epistles. I doubt very much whether any of their writers had any idea that he was writing "Holy Scripture". For the most part of it was "*ad hoc*" writing: a particular situation, or even the behaviour of a particular person or group, called for the writing of the letter. Yet all of them from their different points of view, bear witness to the growing of a new society of men and women quite different from the Greek, Roman, Jewish or pagan pattern. The whole movement is based on the fact (about which no New Testament writer argues) that Jesus Christ was God and man. He is now "the Lord", and every system of thinking and every way of action must be decided not merely by reference to his example and teaching but by the leading of his active living Spirit.

THE STRENGTH OF CONCERTED EVIDENCE

As I continued this close association with the New Testament Epistles (on one full morning each week, for there was plenty of other work to be done!), I found an extraordinary unanimity of spirit. I say "extraordinary" because superficially Paul, James, John and Peter are poles apart in temperament, and widely different in their presentation of the Christian Gospel. But this difference is only superficial: it soon becomes plain that they are all speaking of the same thing and, further, that their messages are complementary rather than contradictory. I have heard professing Christians of our own day speak as though the historicity of the Gospels does not matter — all that matters is the contemporary Spirit of Christ. I contend that the historicity *does* matter, and I do not see why we, who live nearly two thousand years later, should call into question an Event for which there were many eye-witnesses still living at the time when most of the New

Testament was written. It was no "cunningly devised fable" but an historic irruption of God into human history which gave birth to a young Church so sturdy that the pagan world could not stifle or destroy it.

SOME RE-DISCOVERIES

As this New Testament world became more and more real to me, I found several facets of the faith which were bright and shining then but which have become dulled and obscure in our modern discipleship. The first is what Paul calls the "mystery" which has been hidden through all the ages until that time. (Col. 1 : 26). It is simply that Christ lives *in* the personality of the man who believes in him, and brings with him the hope of "glory" to come. No other religion dares to say such a thing about the Person whom men worship as God. God had always been *external*, the Power to be obeyed. Now at last the wonder which we should never have had the impertinence to claim, is seen to have come true in Christ. Not only has God become man and lived life on human terms; not only has God reconciled man to himself by a personal act; not only has God proved that death is conquered by an unforgettable demonstration of power, but God lives *in* the man whose personality is open to him. Life is a matter not of conforming to external rules but of being transformed from within.

THE GOD WITHIN US

This truth, which is mentioned again and again in the New Testament, seems to us too good to be true. We labour and strive and pray as though Christianity were a difficult *performance*. Theoretically we would agree with the notion of the "indwelling Christ", but most of us for most of the time act as though we did not. We have lost sight of the fact that Christ is *in us*, both willing and doing. Consequently we lack that joy, confidence and spontaneity which rightly belongs to the sons of God. This does not, naturally, make our path smooth and free from trouble – neither Jesus nor Paul lived that kind of life. But it makes a whole world of difference when we believe that God, the whole unimaginable power, love and wisdom behind everything, is not merely on our side but actually at work in our hearts and minds.

Of course we believe this in part, and we in the Anglican Church make a special effort to believe it at such times as Confirmation, when the Holy Spirit is imparted to the kneeling confirmand by the laying on of the Bishop's hands. But, alas, how few appear to retain their faith in this super-human happening even for a few months! I blame no one, for I am also a priest and know how difficult it is to communicate a truth at once so simple and so profound.

But how far removed from the idea of the New Testament are the insipid words of the hymn which says "he came sweet influence to impart, a gracious willing guest", and goes on to say, "and his that gentle voice we hear soft as the breath of even, that checks each fault, that calms each fear . . ." Anyone who has any experience at all of the living God knows that he is nothing at all like this: somebody who tut-tuts politely at our failings and lays a soothing hand upon our anxious little heads. The God who lives in us if we allow him, is not necessarily always gentle: he can be wind and fire and a whole lot of other things. He can give us strength, but he can also show us our weakness! He will "increase our faith", but frequently not in the way we want or expect. He will show us, as we can bear it, more and more truth, but he will shatter our illusions without scruple, perhaps especially illusions about ourselves. He will give us moments of wonderful perception, but will also allow us to endure terrifying darkness. His dealings with us are not some optional religious game; he is in deadly earnest and he is intent on "bringing many sons to glory". He is indeed all goodness and light but he will show no more compunction towards the evil things that we have allowed to grow in our hearts than a human surgeon would to a malignant growth. The men of old were hardly exaggerating when they said, "Our God is a consuming fire".

THE IMAGINED GOD — AND THE REAL

I suspect that in our pride we would prefer to have an external God, i.e. one who makes unreasonable demands on us and fails to keep what seems to be the one elementary rule for God – that if we lead good lives we shall (by right) be protected from all the painful and nasty things that happen to other people. It is an easy step from this to atheism. God having plainly failed and we having plainly outgrown him, then we must fall back on ourselves.

Yes, we must, but we do not thereby escape our dealings with God, for it is here in ourselves, that he will, given half a chance, come to live and start putting our house in order! A little bit of us wants this, and a big babyish part of us does not: it refuses to grow up. We would rather be men with a grievance against an imaginary God than have any truck with the real, living God, who, if once we allowed him in, might get up to all sorts of things.

Yes, indeed he might, but we are both wrong and foolish to be afraid. For one thing we cannot in the long run win any battle against the unceasing pressure of God's love, and for another he who appears to be our enemy is not merely our friend but someone who is in closest harmony with our deepest self. "We are not," said Von Hügel, "to think of the Holy Spirit and the human spirit, God and the soul, as two separate entities. God's Spirit works in closest associations with ours."* And in any case, although God may hurt us, he will never harm us, since his nature is Love of the highest kind.

* Quoted by H. A. Williams on p. 18 of *The True Wilderness*.

"THE LIVING GOD" POTENT AND CONTEMPORARY

It seemed, and seems, to me that in the New Testament we have men and women whose lives have been invaded by the living Spirit of God. They are not thereby made instantaneously perfect, as we can see and as they would be the first to admit. But they *are* being transformed and they *are* aware of their new relationship with God and with one another. I cannot believe that this wonderful new factor in human living – and I must underline its newness – was meant to taper off and disappear as the years passed. It is surely part of the everlasting Gospel that God lives and works *in* a man, whether he lives in the first or the twentieth century. It is part of our incredible modern blindness that we fail to see this as the best of good news! And such is the prevailing de-Godded atmosphere that most men see no need for the Gospel at all, and even Christians to some degree miss the wonder of the divine invasion.

I think this sense of the reality of God, both in himself, so to speak, and at work so plainly in human beings is perhaps the great fascination of the New Testament. It may make us wistful; we may long to warm our hands at the fires that are blazing there. It may make us determined to break the tyranny of modern thought-forms which have set such disastrous limits upon our powers of belief. But at least, if we are as honest and as unprejudiced as possible, we are obliged to admit that here is authentic, unpretentious writing, describing in almost everyday terms what to us is a most unlikely miracle — the transformation of human character by the entrance of the love of God. Here is the first and most deadly casualty in our modern pattern of thought: that we do not seriously believe that God is willing to penetrate the inner springs of human character and begin a salutary revolution there. This disbelief is our incalculable loss.

THE PRESENT REALITY OF EVIL

The second difference between New Testament thinking and that of our day is that the powers of evil whether outside or inside the human personality, are never nowadays taken to have any real existence. We willingly admit to being maladjusted or repressed or deprived, and we are quite willing to have psychiatry explain our delinquencies and sins, but we do not usually admit the existence of "evil". Now to men like Paul, John, Peter and James right and wrong existed as surely as light and darkness. The Christian's way was a tough and difficult battle and to win it he needed "the whole armour of God". Theirs was a spiritual struggle against the unseen forces of evil.

If we talk or preach today about the reality of evil we are accused of "Dualism", which is a technical term meaning that this world has really two gods, the God who is all that is good, and Satan who is all that is evil. If our critics mean that we believe in the permanent existence of Satan, the Devil or the powers of evil, they are wrong, for we do not. Once we have passed from this stage of existence into the one Christ has prepared for us "Satan" ceases to exist. But for the time being the power of evil to obstruct, confuse, corrupt, seduce, dissuade — all the unholy battery by which the Christian is assailed — is real, and is to be fought and defeated.

If someone cannot grasp how a fact of this life can cease to be a fact in some other mode of existence, we need look no further for an illustration than our own bodies. For the time being they are real enough, and we must feed and clothe and wash and generally look after them. No one but a madman believes that his body has no reality, and even the strictest ascetic has to eat and drink unless he is bent on suicide. These bodies are real, but only temporarily so. As we have already seen, they are doomed to physical dissolution sooner or later. In another world they cease to be. So it is with the powers of evil. They are "temporary" in the sense that they are limited to this life, but to regard them as anything less than real in the here-and-now can be most dangerous.

All this is nonsense to the uncommitted agnostic, but it is sober truth to the man who is honestly committed to the way of Christ. I have never yet met a Christian who was not tempted, sometimes severely and for a long time, and I don't think I have ever met an agnostic who has any idea of what we mean by our battle against spiritual powers of evil. The New Testament view makes better sense to me than the best of humanism, as well as describing something far more like my own experience and that of the Christians I know. There *is* a struggle, sometimes a very bitter and difficult one, and it is not merely against "absence of good" or "ignorance" or "the amoral unconscious mind". Maybe it is against these, but the sense of conflct against actual evil which the Christian has to fight is as real in his experience as any other part of his observed existence.

THE REALITY OF TEMPTATION

Jesus apparently spoke of "Satan", "the Devil", "the prince of this world" and "the wicked one". Paul wrote of "Satan", "the god of this world", "the devil" and in the famous sixth chapter of his Letter to the Ephesians he speaks of the battle of the Christian "against principalities, against powers, against the rulers of the darkness of this world, against spiritual wickedness in high places". Peter warned his readers that their "adversary the devil, as a roaring lion, walketh about, seeking whom he may devour". James gave the advice to "resist the devil, and he will flee from you". John refers several times to "the devil", the "children of the devil" and "the works of the devil", and, in speaking of the Christian's battle, he reminds his readers that "greater is he that is in you than he that is in the world".

There is no need at all for us to revert to medieval crudity and to conjure up a whole picture-gallery of devils. But it is quite as unrealistic to suppose that there is no adversary, no sower of doubts and fears, no tempter to corrupt our best endeavours. Jesus used the name Satan for this evil force, presumably because it was current in his day and his hearers would know what he was talking about. But, just as he never argued about the existence of God, so he accepted as a fact of life this evil power which can, at any time, destroy or corrupt. It is noteworthy that when Peter was once inspired to see who Jesus really was, Jesus congratulated him on the insight given to him, and almost at once rebuked him sternly as "Satan", for suggesting a course that would be contrary to the plan of God (Matt. 16: 23). I quote here from a recent book: "Anyone who has ever tried to formulate a private prayer in silence, and in his own heart, will know what I mean by *diabolical interference*. The forces of evil are in opposition to the will of God. And the nearer a man's will approaches God's, the more apparent and stronger and more formidable this opposition is seen to be. It is only when we are going in more or less the same direction as the devil that we are unconscious of any opposition at all."* These sentences are completely true to my own experience of life and to that of my Christian friends and correspondents. The battle of which the New Testament speaks so realistically is still raging, and every Christian finds himself involved in it. This is one more reason why these ancient writings ring so true in modern ears.

---

* *Of Heaven and Hope* by David Bolt (Hodder and Stoughton).

THIS WORLD AND THE NEXT

The third element which sounds strongly throughout the New Testament is the conviction that earthly life is no more than a temporary pilgrimage. Heaven, even though there are no earthly words to describe it, is ever-present in the minds of the inspired writers. The words of Paul, which I have already quoted, succinctly describe their common conviction: "I reckon that the sufferings of this present time are not worthy to be compared with the glory which shall be revealed in us."

To many moderns this sounds almost unbearably naïve – as does any idea of reward or punishment in a future life. We must do good, we are told, for the sake of doing good. Similarly we must not hurt others because it is a bad thing to do so. In either case we must put out of our minds any idea of a life to come – that is pure wishful-thinking and belongs to the romantic infancy of religion.

I believe that by cutting out the whole realm of spiritual reality (of which this little life is a mere outcrop in time and space) we are robbing ourselves of more than we know. Instead of being sons of God with unlimited poten-tialities when our present probation is over, we are merely decent humanists with a possible tinge of Christian piety. We have lost a whole dimension, a dimension which the New Testament either robustly asserts or tacitly assumes to be the true and lasting one. We thereby automatically make most of its truth either meaningless or at best a mythical parable.

PAUL KNEW MORE THAN WE THINK

I believe that the best cure for this peculiar state of mind is to study (or re-study) the Letters and actions of a man like Paul. I myself found as I studied his writings that his mind was far more acute than I had thought, and his imagination quite extraordinary in a man of such immense moral and physical courage. I would further say that we moderns tend to underestimate the intelligence of people like Paul. Because such a man had never seen a bicycle, a typewriter or a television set we, perhaps unconsciously, look down on him as living in some sort of twilight ignorance. We forget that he lived in point of time very close to the historic events described in the New Testament, and that he had plenty of opportunity to check their authenticity from many eye-witnesses. We forget, too, that he knew the philosophies of Greece not merely as text-book subjects but as systems of thought being taught and practised in his day. When he wrote to the Colossians and warned them of "philosophy and vain deceit". he was not being anti-intellectual. He knew from observation as well as from personal knowledge of human beings that philosophy, however attractive intellectually, is sterile and impotent when it comes to changing human disposition.

GOD IS NOT A MAGNIFIED MAN!

The fourth remarkable feature of New Testament thinking is the combining of a sense of the immensity of God's wisdom and power with a sure knowledge of his infinite love for each individual person. Thus what seems to be a particular difficulty to the modern thinker is not so regarded by Paul and the others. It does not seem to them incongruous that the wisdom and love of God should operate on a vast scale towards whole nations or worlds, and at the same time care intimately for each separate human being. We exaggerate the difficulty, for if we are not careful we persist in regarding God as a man magnified to the nth degree. We know very well that in matters of human government, however liberal or benevolent, a man is no more than a unit. The elected power is concerned with the well-being of the community as a whole, and cannot possibly be concerned in any intimate way with any individual life. Unless, therefore, we think seriously of what we mean by "God" we constantly transfer this kind of attitude to our creator. Further, now that we know so much more about the structure of the observable universe, whether in terms of size, speed, power or complexity, men too easily assume that one isolated person cannot possibly matter to the vast mind behind it. Even worse, because a thing is beyond man's imagination he dismisses it as impossible. But the New Testament, as, to be fair, does the Old, insists that God is not man. What is impossible to men is perfectly possible to God. I am not

57

a theologian, and neither, I imagine, are most of my readers, and words are slippery things to use when we are talking about God. But surely the chief glory of the Christian Gospel is to declare the unremitting purpose of God's love towards his whole creation; to declare that God became man both to show how life should be lived and to make reconciliation between the evils that are in man and the perfection which belongs to God; and to overcome man's last and darkest enemy, death. The Gospel also declares that the invisible Spirit of God works in and through human beings whenever and wherever he is allowed to transform and guide.

GOD'S "COMPREHENSIVE" LOVE

We may find it difficult to hold all these thoughts in our minds simultaneously, but they fairly represent the way in which the New Testament writers looked at God, man and life. Paul, for example, with his Jewish upbringing and pharisaic training would have a highly exalted view of the one true God, but after his conversion he also knows that the same God whose wisdom is unsearchable is his Father and he can speak personally and naturally of Jesus Christ as "the Son of God who loved me and gave himself for me". In my experience of people I have found that among committed Christians this "comprehensive" view of God as both the Creator of infinite wisdom and power and as the Father caring deeply for the individual is a quite ordinary phenomenon. It is the agnostic or the would-be atheist who produces and magnifies the intellectual difficulty. No one in his senses would pretend that God is anything but a vast unfathomable mystery, and nothing is more repugnant as well as impertinent than that attitude of over-familiarity which suggests that we are now old enough to talk on equal terms with the Creator. Nevertheless it remains true that a human being can in a real sense "know" God through Christ, and Christ himself can be truly alive to him. I have seen this recognition and knowledge of God in people of all denominations, in men and women of several different nationalities as well as in those who belong to various social strata. I have known extremely clever scientists as well as men of the highest calibre in literature or the arts who regard God with the deepest awe and at the same time know him through Christ almost as a personal friend. I have also known people of a much simpler cast of mind, who would probably not be able to pass any formal examination, who have a sturdy and invincible faith in God their Father and similarly find Christ a real person. It is true that the comparatively unintelligent will sometimes use naïve terms in speaking of God, but I have never found a true Christian without a profound sense of awe and wonder. I cannot help being impressed by what I have seen and by what people have told me. The laboratory-check for spiritual experience is life itself, and it is exactly here, sometimes in the most appallingly dangerous and painful situations that I have found faith both sure and radiant. In short, I have seen the experience of God described in the New

Testament occurring again and again in our modern world.

THE FOLLY OF TAKING SIMILES LITERALLY

There is an idea current among some New Testament scholars that people like Paul had a primitive system of thought — that theirs was a three-decker universe, with "heaven" above, "hell" below, and "earth" in between. For myself I seriously doubt this. In the intensive reading which translation requires I formed the strong impression that so far from trying to fit ideas of God into any preconceived concept, Paul is struggling with human words to express something of the wonders which, he senses, lie beyond observable life. To him it is the things which are seen which are temporal; it is the unseen things which are eternal. I find it hard to be patient with modern critics who assume that when Paul speaks of Christ's ascending "up on high" or when he urges the Colossians to "seek those things which are above, where Christ sitteth at the right hand of God", he is really talking of some location a certain number of miles above the earth's surface. There is a disquieting confusion of thought here. I think I can understand the Russian astronaut who is reputed to have said on his return from orbit that now he knew that there was no God since he had been out in space and there was no one there. This shows merely a peasant's-eye view of religion. But there are several modern writers who pour scorn upon any idea of God being *up* or *above*.

They are confusing literal spatial position with a mental image which must be common to nearly all thinking human beings. Why should we talk of *high* ideals or a *high* purpose? Why should we talk of a *rise* in salary? Why should sales be *soaring*? Why should a boy be promoted from the *Lower* to the *Upper* Vth form? Why does an important person in our judiciary sit in a *high* court? And so we could go on. It is a common and quite understandably symbolic way of speaking, and naturally the converse of it is equally true. For example in ordinary speech a man may *fall* in our estimation, a failing business is fast going *downhill*, some people are of *low* intelligence and some unfortunates have sunk to the *depths*, etc.

As I studied Paul's Letters I became convinced that he uses expressions of height and depth as useful symbols but not as geographical locations. When, for example, he writes that "God raised Christ from the dead and set him at his own right hand in the heavenly places, far above all principality and power, and might, and dominion, and every name that is named, not only in this world, but also in that which is to come", does anyone seriously imagine that Paul, or the Ephesian Christians to whom he was writing, thought of this exaltation as being measurable in physical terms? Again, in the same Letter to Ephesus, when Paul asserts that the Christian's real battle is against spiritual rather than physical enemies and mentions "spiritual wickedness in high places", does anyone seriously suggest that Paul meant demonic goings-on at the Emperor's court? Of course not! To Paul there was the heavenly reality which at present we may sense but not see, and the earthly reality which is discernible by the senses but doomed, like all creation, to ultimate decay. The "bright blue sky" stuff belongs to Victorian piety and not to the New Testament.

THE NECESSITY FOR PICTURE-LANGUAGE

I feel I must record here my sense of injustice that the Christian religion should be singled out as a target for criticism because it uses, and is bound to use, "picture-language". We all do it every day of our lives, and we are none the worse for it. No one blames the accountant for talking of a "balance", the economist for speaking of "frozen assets", the electronics engineer for talking of a magnetic "field", the traffic controller for referring to a "peak" period, the electrical engineer for speaking of "load-shedding" or the town-planner for talking of a "bottle-neck". Not one of these words is literally true but each conveys quickly, and pretty accurately, an idea which can be readily understood. I cannot see why we, who accept hundreds of such usages in everyday speaking and writing, should decide that an expression such as "seated at the right hand of the Father" is either literally true or totally false.

But just as there is a real situation behind each of the shorthand "pictures" which I have given above so there is a reality behind every Christian expression. Because picture-language is sometimes used it does not follow that the actual events are unhistorical or "mythical". The strange thing to me is that so few New Testament expressions need explanation. There are obvious exceptions: the Epistle to the Hebrews was especially written for the Hebrew mind and necessarily contains many ideas and expressions which are strange to the non-Jew. But on the whole the technical expressions are few and the "pictures" easily understood. Given a good translation, there is little in the New Testament letters which the modern reader will find dated or irrelevant. Indeed, as I said in a slightly different context above, I have literally hundreds of letters written from all parts of the English-speaking world which prove this very point. And although the difficulties are very much greater, those who have, with enormous care and sympathy, translated the Epistles into many other languages have found a similar response. The British and the American Bible Societies have an impressive record of the relevance of the New Testament Epistles to life as people of very different backgrounds and cultures have to live it today.

SOME UNEXPECTED DISCOVERIES

Just over two hundred years ago, in 1754 to be precise, Horace Walpole coined the word "serendipity" which has now come to be accepted into our language. The word, which is derived from the ancient name for Ceylon, is defined as "the faculty of making happy and unexpected discoveries by accident". Before I go on to discuss the work of translating the Gospels I feel I must mention

E

some of the "happy and unexpected discoveries" which I made in the translation of the Epistles.

SERENDIPITY: 1

The first one I will mention, which of course may all the time have been no secret to anybody else, was the expression "rich in mercy". (Eph. 2: 4). This struck me as a positive jewel. Just as we might say that a Texas tycoon is "rich in oil", so Paul writes it as a matter of fact that God is "rich in mercy". The pagan world was full of fear, and the Christian Gospel set out to replace that fear of the gods or the fates, or even life itself, with love for and trust in God. "Rich in mercy" was Good News to the ancient world and it is Good News today.

SERENDIPITY: 2

I think the idea of God's personal care for the individual came upon me with a similar unexpected strength when I came to translate 1 Peter 5: 7, which reads in the Authorised Version "casting all your care upon him; for he careth for you". In one sense it is quite plain that God wants us to bear responsibility; it is a false religion which teaches that God wants us to be permanently immature. But there is a sense in which the conscientious and the imaginative can be overburdened. This familiar text reminded me that such over-anxiety can be "off-loaded" on to God for each one of us is his personal concern. The "text" is commonplace enough, perhaps too commonplace, for it was not until I had to translate it that I came to realise something of its full force. The word used for "casting" is an almost violent word, conveying the way in which a man at the end of his tether might throw aside an intolerable burden. And the Christian is recommended to throw this humanly insupportable weight upon the only one who can bear it and at the same time to realise that God cares for him intimately as a person. "He careth for you" is hardly strong enough and I don't know that I did much better in rendering the words "you are his personal concern". The Greek words certainly mean this but probably more. It is not the least glory of the Christian Gospel that the God revealed by Jesus Christ possesses wisdom and power beyond all human imagining but never loses sight of any individual human being. It may seem strange to us and it may seem an idea quite beyond our little minds to comprehend, but each one of us *matters* to God. It is of course the same sense of intimate concern which Jesus expressed poetically when he assured us that even the hairs on our head are numbered. It is the kind of inspired truth of which we have continually to remind ourselves, if only because life so often apparently contradicts it.

SERENDIPITY: 3

I had for some time been worried about the expression "fear and trembling". It did not seem likely to me that Paul in writing to the Philippians could have meant literally that they were to work out their salvation in a condition of anxiety and nervousness. We all know that fear destroys love and spoils relationships, and a great deal of the New Testament is taken up with getting rid of the old ideas of fear and substituting the new ideas of love and trust. I realised that the Greek word translated "fear" can equally well mean "reverence" or "awe" or even "respect", but I was bothered about the "trembling". Surely the same Spirit who inspired Paul to write to Timothy that "God hath not given us the spirit of fear; but of power, and of love, and of a sound mind" could not also have meant us to live our entire lives in a state of nervous terror. I came to the conclusion, a little reluctantly, that the expression "in fear and trembling" had become a bit of a cliché, even as it has in some circles today. As I went on translating I found that this must be the case. For when Paul wrote to the Corinthians and reported that Titus had been encouraged and refreshed by their reception of him, he then goes on to say that the Corinthian Christians received him with "fear and trembling"! (2 Cor. 7: 15). Now this makes nonsense, unless it is a purely conventional verbal form implying proper respect. For, little as we know of Titus, we cannot imagine any real Christian minister being encouraged and re-

freshed by a display of nervous anxiety. We get the same
phrase occurring again in Paul's advice to Christian slaves
(Eph. 6: 5), where the context makes it quite clear that
faithfulness and responsibility are much more what Paul
means than "fear and trembling". This much became
plain, and then I realised that when Paul really did mean
the words to be taken literally he amplified them to make
sure they would be properly understood. I think we sometimes imagine that the incredibly heroic Paul suffered from
no human weaknesses, except for the "thorn in the flesh"
about which all New Testament commentators have
written. (2 Cor. 12: 7). But if we turn to 1 Cor. 2: 3 we
find Paul writing that "I was with you in weakness, and
in fear, and in much trembling". Now this is a different
thing altogether. Here we have a man honest enough to
admit that he was frightened and that he was, or had been,
ill. "Fear and trembling" here are perfectly legitimate. It
is only when they are used as a phrase almost without
literal meaning that we begin to feel uncomfortable.

SERENDIPITY: 4

This leads me on to another heartening discovery, which
I made in 2. Cor. 1: 8ff. I had not previously realised that
even a man of such indomitable courage as Paul, filled as
he undoubtedly was with the Spirit of the living God,
could nevertheless be "pressed out of measure, above
strength, insomuch that we despaired even of life". We
lesser mortals, who live infinitely less adventurous lives,

may sometimes experience something of this pressure. It is not that we, any more than Paul, despair of God as far as the ultimate outcome is concerned. But we can be overcome by the most terrifying darkness and reduced to a sense of inadequacy amounting to near desperation. Again, it was not until I came to the close study of this passage that I realised under what fearful pressure Paul must at times have been. I further came to see that the "stiff upper lip" business is not necessarily Christian; it sounds much more like a throw-back to the Stoics than to early Christianity. For although the New Testament abounds in advice to men to be strong and to master their fears, it does not consider it disgraceful, for example, that a man might be moved even to tears, not indeed for himself but because he cared deeply for others. The Letters tell no story of idealised human beings but reflect the life of people who are changed but by no means yet perfect.

SERENDIPITY: *5*

At some stage in my life as a Christian I must have heard the total depravity of man heavily emphasised. I do not think I ever personally accepted this, because ordinary observation showed a good deal of kindness and generosity produced by people whether they had religious faith or not. But I have found among gatherings of Christians of various denominations a minority who seemed to get a perverse delight in this emphasis on man's utter hopelessness. And indeed we have not got to look far into devotional literature, whether Protestant or Catholic, to come across the idea that man is hopelessly sinful and incapable of good without the operation of the grace of God. I am not at all proud of Article 13 in the Book of Common Prayer which says the same thing in a peculiarly unpleasant way. Now, to my joy, I found two delightful instances which could be quoted against the detractors of humanity if, as they sometimes do, they want to indulge in a text-slanging match! One comes from the first Epistle of John where the writer reminds his hearers that no one should deceive them by any clever talk, "The man who lives a consistently good life is a good man as surely as God is good". This truth is no more and no less than the saying of Christ himself when he said, "you will recognise them by their fruit; a good tree cannot produce bad fruit, any more than a bad tree can produce good fruit." This was a pleasant refreshment, but there was another wholly unexpected one at the end of the first Epistle to the Corinthians (16: 13), where Paul urges his converts in the words "Quit you like men". (May I say in passing that these words from the Authorised Version are totally meaningless to the vast majority of young people.) The literal translation is of course, "Be *men*". Now if it is true that man is so steeped in iniquity and incapable of goodness as some, especially in past centuries, would have us believe, there is no sense whatever in Paul's advice. But if it is true that the image of God is still present in man, however much it has been distorted or disfigured by evil, then it makes the most encouraging sense to be told to live like a man. At any rate I must put it on record that this is the effect the inspired words had upon me.

SERENDIPITY: 6

A similar pleasant "discovery" came in 1 John 4: 7 in the words, "everyone that loveth is born of God, and knoweth God". Again, this inspired truth had naturally been there all the time, but I don't think I had ever heard a sermon preached on it. Throughout my years of experience it had struck me that the things that were really admirable in human behaviour were those inspired by love. I had also noticed, like many others, that people could exhibit most remarkable compassionate love without any great religious profession, or indeed with none at all. But if it is true, as John declares, that "God is love" it would make sense that any action which sprang from love had its origin in God. It would also mean that those who did give themselves in love to others did in fact "know God", however loudly they might protest their agnosticism. I have never been happy with any ecclesiastical or theological system in which correctness of belief was of paramount importance. It is only too easy for some men to build up a certain theological structure which includes them and excludes others. But what we really believe in our hearts of hearts may be quite different from what we outwardly profess. I saw then, and I have seen nothing in life to disturb this view, that when a man acts in response to love and compassion he is responding to God *whatever he thinks or says.* Conversely the man who refuses to become involved in the troubles and burdens of his fellows is rejecting God, however religious his outward profession may be.

SERENDIPITY: 7

"Beloved", wrote John, "now are we the sons of God, and it doth not yet appear what we shall be: but we know that, when he shall appear, we shall be like him; for we shall see him as he is." (1 John 3:2). These words, familiar as I think they must have been to me for years, were yet another shock for me as I came to translate them. For what would normally be sheer effrontery or even blasphemy is here written with cool confidence and authority. No one to my knowledge has ever written like these New Testament writers. Yet I was constantly aware that I was dealing not with exhortations or homilies but with letters written to people living in the midst of this world's business, people who were tempted and tried as we are, blinkered and frustrated and limited just as we are, yet with the same unquenchable flame of hope in their hearts as Christians have today. The material in this single verse is quite extraordinarily compressed; there is enough here for half a dozen useful sermons! But it is the *authority* which stabs the spirit broad awake. Paul and John wrote because they *knew*. The Christian revelation was not to them a tentative hypothesis, but the truth about God and men. They had known it by experience, and seen it demonstrated as a powerful force in the lives of men. The whole Christian pattern had to be lived against pagan darkness and frequently overt hostility. It required super-human qualities to survive. Of course there were casualties — Demas was not the first nor the last deserter — but the amazing thing to me is that the Christian Gospel took root and flourished in many different, and indeed unlikely, places.

SERENDIPITY: 8

There was another unexpected treasure waiting for me in the Letter of James. I suppose we all look upon the many disappointments and pains of this life as somehow hostile to us. We either fight or we grimly endure. It was there-fore a salutary surprise to me to discover that James recommends his Christian brothers to *welcome* the assorted trials and trouble to which we are all exposed. "Count it all joy" he writes "when ye fall into divers [=all kinds of] temptations." (1:2). Frankly I had never even thought of thus turning our apparent losses into real gains! But I am convinced that it is the right attitude to adopt. This is no question of "being a martyr", as we said when we were children, but of accepting suffering and loss as an integral part of life. I think we moderns are influenced more than we know by current modes of thinking which assume that we have a "right" to be happy, a "right" to live without pain and somehow a "right" to be shielded from the ills which flesh is heir to. Evidently the early

Christians thought no such thing. They quite plainly took it as an honour to suffer for Christ's sake, and here the advice is to accept all kinds of troubles, whether they are apparently for Christ's sake or not, as friends instead of resenting them as intruders. Now I know that this kind of teaching can easily degenerate into an unhealthy and perverse wallowing in trouble. But this is not, I think, the early Christian intention. It is just as much a Christian duty to rejoice with those who rejoice as it is to weep with those who weep; it is as important to enjoy what God has richly given to us as it is to accept good humouredly and patiently the troubles, set-backs, disappointments and griefs which are also part of the human pattern.

SERENDIPITY: 9

There are naturally many more happy and unexpected discoveries which I made over the years, some of them perhaps merely revealing how superficial must have been my previous knowledge of the New Testament Letters. But since this is a personal testimony, I have felt it right to mention some of the things which came to me with fresh and startling clarity. I have kept the best until last. It occurs in 1 John 3: 20. Like many others, I find myself something of a perfectionist, and if we don't watch ourselves this obsession for the perfect can make us arrogantly critical of other people, and in certain moods, desperately critical of ourselves. In this state of mind it is not really that I cannot subscribe to the doctrine of the

73

Forgiveness of Sins, but that the tyrannical super-Me condemns and has no mercy on myself. Now, John, in his wisdom, points out in these inspired words, "if our heart condemn us, God is greater than our heart, and knoweth all things". This is a gentle but salutary rebuke to our assumption that we know better than God! God, on any showing, is infinitely greater in wisdom and love than we are, and, unlike us, knows all the factors involved in human behaviour. We are guilty of certain things and these we must confess with all honesty and make reparation where possible. But there may be many factors in our lives for which we are not really to blame at all. We did not choose our heredity; we did not choose the bad, indifferent or excellent way in which we were brought up. This is naturally not to say that every wrong thing we do, or every fear or rage to which we are subject today, is due entirely to heredity, environment and upbringing. But it certainly does mean that we are in no position to judge ourselves; we simply must leave that to God who is our Father and "is greater than our heart and knoweth all things". It is almost as if John is saying, "if God loves us, who are we to be so high and mighty as to refuse to love ourselves?"

3. The Truth of the Gospels

I HAVE so far been writing chiefly of my translation of the Epistles. I hesitated long before I entered the world of the Gospels. In retrospect I think this was largely due to natural caution. I could apparently, by dint of hard thinking and sympathy with both New Testament Greek and the twentieth-century reader, convey something of the electric energy of the Letters. I was not aiming so much at absolute accuracy as to try to produce in modern minds what I imagined the original Greek words produced in the minds of first century readers and hearers. But while I felt at liberty to disentangle some of Paul's complex arguments, or to paraphrase where direct translation would not make sense, I was not at all sure that I could find the same success in rendering the four Gospels into modern English. The problem was in many ways more difficult. For the most part the Gospels are straightforward narrative, and although there are obscurities and archaisms the general effect of the Authorised Version is one of simple beauty. I could not, and did not try to, rival that wonderful translation of 1611. I simply "forgot" as completely as I could familiar words and turns of phrase and translated the first century Greek into what

75

I thought would be its modern equivalent in English.

I have already referred to my rather snobbish approach to New Testament Greek which had seemed to me poor in vocabulary, loose in construction and generally of small literary value. I have since revised that opinion considerably, but at the time of translation the overwhelming feeling was one of their true inspiration. I did not find myself worried by a rather uncertain chronology, or even by apparent discrepancies between the various accounts. But I was intensely conscious of the enormous importance of what was being described in these seemingly artless pages.

AN INTERVIEW WITH A FELLOW-TRANSLATOR

Some years before the publication of the New English Bible I was invited by the B.B.C. to discuss the problems of translation with Dr. E. V. Rieu, who had himself recently produced a translation of the four Gospels for Penguin Classics. Towards the end of the discussion Dr. Rieu was asked about his general approach to the task, and his reply was this:

"My personal reason for doing this was my own intense desire to satisfy myself as to the authenticity and the spiritual content of the Gospels. And, if I received any new light by an intensive study of the Greek originals, to pass it on to others. I approached them in the same spirit as I would have approached them had they been presented to me as recently discovered Greek manuscripts."

A few minutes later I asked him, "Did you get the feeling that the whole material is extraordinarily alive? —I got the feeling that the whole thing was alive even while one was translating. Even though one did a dozen versions of a particular passage, it was still living. Did you get that feeling?" Dr. Rieu replied: "I got the deepest feeling that I possibly could have expected. It—changed me; my work changed me. And I came to the conclusion that these words bear the seal of—the Son of Man and God. And they're the Magna Carta of the human spirit."

I found it particularly thrilling to hear a man who is a scholar of the first rank as well as a man of wisdom and experience openly admitting that these words written long ago were alive with power. They bore to him, as to me, the ring of truth.

WHAT ARE THE "GOSPELS"?

The Gospels are not, in the modern sense, biographies. We have no idea of the physical stature or build of their chief subject, and no clue to his colouring. We do not know whether he had a powerful voice, although we may fairly infer that he was physically strong. Apart from one isolated incident, we have no information about his childhood, adolescence or young manhood and no record of the influences which formed his character. If we are looking for biography in the modern sense, we are disappointed. Some, like the late Albert Schweitzer, came to the conclusion that we never could know Jesus as a historical figure. And quite a number of scholars today would hold much the same view. The most we can do is to understand the meaning behind the "myths" of the Hellenic-Semitic world of first century Palestine. I cannot, as a translator, agree with this at all, except in one minor way, which I will return to later.

Suppose you are, as I was, translating with the mind emptied as far as possible of preconception. You cannot help noticing the differences between the hurried, almost breathless, style of Mark where almost everything seems to happen "straightway" and the much more elaborate Gospel of Matthew, who has a very definite purpose in view – to convince the Jews that Jesus was indeed the Messiah of whom the Old Testament prophets had spoken. Quite different again is the work of Luke, who appears to have made diligent research and unearthed some stories of Jesus which none of the other evangelists mention. Here, uniquely, are set down the concern of Jesus for women, for foreigners and for the underprivileged. To me it had all the marks of careful writing. And then came the problematical Fourth Gospel, which is a work of quite different character.

A COMPOSITE PORTRAIT

Suppose that you have spent many hundred hours in putting these four widely differing accounts of some of the sayings and doings of the man Jesus into today's

English. Do you find yourself so confused that you conclude that there was no such person at all? I take leave to doubt it. It is, in my experience, the people who have never troubled seriously to study the four Gospels who are loudest in their protests that there was no such person. I felt, and feel, without any shadow of doubt that close contact with the text of the Gospels builds up in the heart and mind a character of awe-inspiring stature and quality. I have read, in Greek and Latin, scores of myths but I did not find the slightest flavour of myth here. There is no hysteria, no careful working for effect and no attempt at collusion. These are not embroidered tales: the material is cut to the bone. One sensed again and again that understatement which we have been taught to think is more "British" than Oriental. There is an almost childlike candour and simplicity, and the total effect is tremendous. No man could ever have invented such a character as Jesus. No man could have set down such artless and vulnerable accounts as these unless some real Event lay behind them.

Thus the only small point which I will concede to the de-mythologisers is that several times I got the impression that the first three evangelists, naturally enough, did not quite realise what a world-shaking happening they were describing. But how could they? Their view of the world was small; their knowledge of history was limited. They did not know even what Paul knew of contemporary life around them. It is easy for us to feel that these men were ignorant peasants compared with ourselves who have advanced in knowledge over nearly two thousand years. If we do, we underestimate their intelligence and

over-estimate our own. Obviously they could not have anything approaching our historical perspective, but against
this we must set the fact that they were living very much
nearer to the actual point of time when Jesus was alive.
There seems singularly little point in their concocting
mythical stories about someone who never lived when
violent persecution against those who followed the way of
Jesus was well under way.

EVANGELISTS NOT BIOGRAPHERS

When I say that the first three Gospels at any rate are
not biographies in the modern sense at all, I do not mean
to say for one moment that I regard them as untrue. On
the contrary, I believe them to be the verbal distillation of
some of the things which Jesus said and did which the
early evangelists felt constrained to put down in writing.
It is impossible at this stage to say what their original
sources were, and do not let us forget that in no case have
we an original manuscript or anything like it. But from
the major manuscripts, and from the thousands of minor
ones, the textual experts are able to reconstruct with fair
certainty what the evangelists wrote in the first instance.
One thing is perfectly clear: these men were not in a con-
spiracy together or they would have been careful to avoid
minor contradictions and discrepancies. The scholars who
work out with enormous pains, through the evidence of
style and vocabulary as well as from the content, the sources
from which the evangelists worked are called form-critics.

Of course, the whole business of form-criticism is as absorbing and exciting as the best of detective stories, and I think it would surprise the average layman to know, for example, to what lengths the form-critics will go in order to "prove" that some part of Luke's gospel belonged to another period of time, or indeed to another author than the rest of it.

TITLES ARE NOT DIVINELY INSPIRED

I should not like it to be thought that I want to belittle the work of the form-critics, even though I sometimes cannot resist a smile at the way their views have changed over the last thirty years. But to me, as a translator, their work was largely irrelevant. I was dealing with material which was startingly alive, and I could not really be overmuch bothered whether Matthew "borrowed" part of his Gospel story from Mark, or whether he and Mark shared a common source of written or spoken information which the critics call "Q". I know it is a shock to us today, and perhaps especially if we are professional writers and conscious of the laws of copyright, but it was not in the least strange in the first century A.D. to say that a gospel was "according to Matthew", even though it might contain sentences which were not written by Matthew at all. As long as the incident or the teaching was in keeping with the main stream which he had established, it seemed perfectly all right to the early Church to include it under Matthew's name. Perhaps the nearest we can get to

81

understanding this in modern times is to consider standard works of reference. We may possess *Crockford's Clerical Directory*, but we do not expect it to be compiled by a man called Crockford today. We may have a general work of reference called *Whitaker's Almanack*. We rely on the name Whitaker to give the work integrity and reliability, but we do not expect there to be a living Whitaker who wrote every word of this year's edition.

THE RETENTIVE ORIENTAL MIND

What seems to have happened, and in this I think all Christian scholars agree, is that the first three evangelists wrote down what had previously been an oral tradition. This is no more than intelligent guesswork, but it seems likely that in the early days of the Christian community there was no need to write down the stories of what Jesus said and did, especially as many of them were apparently expecting his early personal return. But what is not a guess but a fact is the fantastic retentiveness of the oriental mind. Stories are told by word of mouth again and again, and no verbal deviation or embellishment is allowed. It is a phenomenon rather like that which children exhibit when they are very young and have their favourite bed-time story. It must not vary in the slightest detail from the familiar pattern. Strangely enough only this very year I have been in contact with a friend who worked for some twenty-five years in business in Malaya. He found to his astonishment that conversations of twenty years ago and

more, could be recalled perfectly, mistakes, faulty pro-
nunciations and all, even though he himself had forgotten
everything but the merest outline of such talk. Now this
I am told would have been true of the Mediterranean
world, and to me it seems most likely that it is the recol-
lection of certain gems of speech and actions of Jesus
which the first three evangelists record. This would account for the loose chronology, for we are reading not
history in the modern sense but events and sayings
treasured and remembered over a generation.

If we accept that the evangelists, or at any rate the first
three, wrote down various oral traditions which had been
passed on with scrupulous accuracy over the years, we
shall be spared many unnecessary headaches. Is it not
reasonable to suppose that Jesus gave his teaching in
slightly different forms on various occasions to differing
groups of people and that these were separately remembered and cherished? Before the days of mass communication (and that is not long ago) the prophet, preacher
or politician was bound to repeat his message again and
again. What he said would be couched in compressed,
intelligible and memorable terms, but no one need suppose that he always used precisely the same words with
parrot-like precision.

THE EVANGELISTS ARE NOT "REPORTERS"

It is probably that Jesus spoke in Aramaic (a popular form
of Hebrew), and if this is so then the evangelists had the

extremely difficult job of listening to slightly varying accounts of the same, or similar, incidents and then setting them down in the widely-understood Greek of the time. They were not reporters in the modern sense, nor were they preparing a statement for any court of law. They were simply setting down in writing what had till then been memorised and repeated by word of mouth. It is highly unlikely that we shall get any more information about the life and teaching of Jesus than we have already. In a sense this is tantalising; what would we not give for a full-scale biography of this extraordinary man? How immensely valuable would be accurate descriptions of all that he ever said, as well as a detailed account of the events of his life. Why, we may plaintively ask, are we left almost completely in the dark about the childhood and young manhood of Jesus? Why have we no information (which would be regarded as essential in any modern biography), about the formative influences which produced such a matchless character? Why do we know almost nothing of the period between what we commonly call the resurrection and the ascension? What was it that the now risen Christ then taught to his followers about the "things pertaining to the kingdom", as Luke describes them with such maddening brevity in the first chapter of "The Acts"? The plain answer is that we do not know.

The discovery of many *papyri* written in the same kind of Greek as the New Testament has certainly illuminated our understanding of many words and expressions of that time. The Dead Sea Scrolls may well fill in more of our knowledge of Palestinian life of about the time of Jesus.

But it seems to me unlikely that the small esoteric group who copied and preserved the scrolls will shed any fresh light upon the actual historic life of Jesus or even, as some suggest, of John the Baptist.

THE AUTHORITY OF JOHN'S GOSPEL

This is not the place to write at any length about the Fourth Gospel. It is different in style, in vocabulary and in "atmosphere". Instead of the true nature of Jesus being discovered in the course of his ministry it is asserted at the beginning. Almost the whole of the story is set in Jerusalem. There is little mention of the extensive healing ministry of mind and body which the first three evangelists record. Instead of short parables we have quite lengthy discourses. There are times (inevitably, since New Testament Greek did not use quotation marks), when we are not sure whether we are reading the remembered words of Jesus himself or the comment of the evangelist. Nevertheless the impact of the whole Gospel is, one is tempted to say, greater than the other three put together. The author plainly knew Jesus and had had time to think and meditate on the significance of the "Word becoming flesh". Whether he knew the existing Gospels we do not know, but I did not get the impression that John was writing a deliberate correction. The feeling is that a man of more maturity and deeper insight is giving his account. He is in effect saying "This is how I saw and heard Jesus Christ and this is the significance of his

85

coming to this earth". The result is the portrait of a character in no way different from the sketches supplied by Matthew, Mark and Luke but carrying an even deeper authority.

Naturally I have read a good number of commentaries on John's Gospel, and I am fairly familiar with the difficulties of deciding who was the author. I also know of the hard task awaiting anyone who tries to fit this work into a "harmony" with the other Gospels. But I was not primarily concerned with this sort of thing. My work was to translate for, not to confuse, the modern reader.

4. The Truth of Jesus

THE STRENGTH OF JESUS AS A MAN

WHAT happened to me as the work progressed was that the figure of Jesus emerged more and more clearly, and in a way unexpectedly. Of course I had a deep respect, indeed a great reverence for the conventional Jesus Christ whom the Church worshipped. But I was not at all prepared for the *unconventional* man revealed in these terse Gospels. No one could possibly have invented such a person: this was no puppet-hero built out of the imaginations of adoring admirers. "This man Jesus" so briefly described, rang true, sometimes alarmingly true. I began to see now why the religious Establishment of those days wanted to get rid of him at all costs. He was sudden death to pride, pomposity and pretence.

This man could be moved with compassion and could be very gentle, but I could find no trace of the "Gentle-Jesus-meek-and-mild". He was quite terrifyingly tough, not in a Bulldog Drummond – James Bond sort of way, but in the sheer strength of a unified and utterly dedicated personality. He once (at least) walked unscathed through a murderous crowd. I have known a few, a very, very few, men who could do that. But then I find that this sheer strength was still his after hours of unspeakable agony in the garden of Gethsemane. Those who were sent to arrest him "fell back to the ground". Previous pious generations attribute this to some supernatural power. I don't believe this for a moment. Jesus was a man of such complete authority that he could remain in command of a situation even when the odds were heavily against him.

JESUS IS MAN, NOT SUPERMAN

It was this strength of human character which struck me again and again. We are not being told of a superman but of someone supremely human. He could work so hard that his followers begged him to stop. Yet he was fast asleep aboard the little fishing-boat while the others did the rowing. He was awake and out praying in solitude while the others were asleep, yet there were times when he was tired. "Jesus, being wearied with his journey, sat down beside a well", records John. He touched the untouchable leper, he made friends with those who had lost their reputation and self-respect. He denounced in vitriolic words the leaders of so-called "religion". He spoke fearlessly to the violently insane. He wept in the presence of human sorrow. He also wept over Jerusalem because its people utterly failed to recognise God's Messiah when he taught and preached among them, and also because with the true prophet's insight he foresaw the city's hideous destruction. Even with a little imaginative sympathy one could sense the agony of his frustration and near-despair. For the first time it seemed to me that it was because he